One Step at a Time

ONE STEP AT A TIME

Walking in the Manifestation of God's Word

DR. ANGELA E. THOMAS-DUPREE

Bro. Cornelius
Thank you for your guidance
and concern for my youngsme (Jason/Justin)
Showers g Blessings

Angela
Thomas-D.

Copyright © 2020 by Dr. Angela E. Thomas-DuPree

One Step at a Time: *Walking in the Manifestation of God's Word.*

ISBN-13: 978-0-578-71818-7

Published by A.E. Thomas-DuPree.

Ft. Lauderdale, FL.

Author website: draethomasdupree.com

Editor: Nakia J.S. Thomas of *Few Editorial & Creative Suite*

This book is dedicated to the readers. As you read this book, you will be encouraged to follow God's will for your dreams and endeavors, no matter the limitations of your present situation.

And to my wisdom sharers, I dedicate this book as an extension of your guiding words:

"Your whole life is a manifestation of the thoughts that go on in your head" (Lisa Nichols). "Fully inhale your dream and completely exhale the manifestation of it" (TF Hodge).

"Tomorrow is the day the Universe will deliver an amazing blessing to you. Get ready. Your manifestation will be a success" (The Law of Attraction).

ACKNOWLEDGEMENTS

We can't survive this life alone. It starts with God. We are molded by God's grace and mercy and the love and contribution of others.

My profound gratitude to my husband Clyde S. DuPree, thank you for your encouragement, support, and love. To my children who always believe in Mommy and gives me their vote of confidence when I grow weary.

To my brothers and sisters who always accept my new endeavors with anticipation. I pay homage to my late father and mother; your soft whispers of guidance are with me every day. Thank you for your firm and consistent guidance.

To my relatives and friends, your words of reassurance fuels my inspiration—to each of you, thank you.

To my dear niece Ms. Nakia J. S. Thomas and her company Few Editorial & Creative Suite, thank you for your assistance, guidance, enthusiasm, and encouragement with this project. Your exemplary professionalism was shown in each phase of this project. I could not have done this without you, with every ounce of gratitude, I thank you and your team.

CONTENTS

PREFACE

May this book give you the insight of God's words in action. Consider what you read from this page forward to be evidence—proof that anything you put your mind to, while staying in harmony with God's word, must come to pass.

God's word is filled with promises. As you read His promises, claim them over your life. Speak them out loud, and you will begin to experience God moving in your life for His glory and your good. God has a plan for your life and that includes plans to prosper you, keep you safe, and give you hope.

For I know the plans I have for you," says the Lord.
"They are plans for good and not for disaster, to give
you a future and a hope.
– Jeremiah 29:11

Many are the plans in the mind of a man, but it is the purpose of the Lord that will stand.
– Proverbs 19:21

Life offers you more when you have your purpose in perspective. Your purpose is what will maneuver you around your challenges, around your pain, and around your current situation. It encourages you beyond what we see in the natural and propels you into the spiritual realm. Whether you have just begun your walk with Christ or starting anew, now is the time to revisit your thoughts and ramp up your daily devotion to experiencing God's manifestation in your life. This book chronicles my walk with God and is intended to assist you in reflecting on your experiences with God on a daily basis.

I pray that you enjoy this short read, and I challenge you to pursue God's direction and guidance as He manifests His grace in your life one step at a time!

But, as it is written, "What no eyes has seen, nor ear heard, nor the heart of man imagined, what God has prepared for those who love Him.
– 2 Corinthians 2:9

The steps of a [woman] are established by the Lord,
when [she] delights in [her] way—
– Psalm 37:23

FOREWORD

I first met Dr. Angela Dupree while serving as the Chaplain of Delta Sigma Theta Sorority, Inc. (South Broward Alumnae Chapter, FL).

I became more familiar with Angela on a service project trip to Bimini. As we perused around the island on the golf cart, she shared how being the last of twelve children impacted her life and pushed her to strive for desires and fulfillments beyond what she could imagine. We laugh a lot when we're together, but she is committed to serving and paying her blessings forward. As we trotted around that island, she was devising a plan on how to provide additional resources to the school. Much of what we saw, reminded us of our humble beginnings in many ways.

In this book, Angela has brought to life another opportunity to learn of God's faithful covenant over us through faith. Teachings around trusting and believing God for all things through the powerful words of scripture continues to resonate from within. It is a common thread intertwined in her soul, from her early years into the present.

The stories within this book are testaments to those who feel the road is closed to a select group, due to barriers unseen or unknown. It will challenge you to press toward the mark of the prize of the high calling of God in Christ Jesus. (Philippians 3:14). It will grant permission to fight the odds and reach for your highest level of potential, making no apologies for your success.

I believe you will also be encouraged to share this work with others because of the simplicity of the writing, as well as the depth and passion felt through her faith. While many have known Dr. Angela Dupree far longer than me, I am honored to call her sister, and I would like to express my gratitude to her for trusting me to share my thoughts.

Accomplishing God's purpose and plans for our lives and being conformed to the character of Christ is our ultimate goal.

Rev. Stephanie Bevill
Angela's Sister-in-Christ

INTRODUCTION

After meeting Ms. Oprah Winfrey in October of 2014 and then religiously watching her "Master Class" shows, I was inspired to write this book. Her opening statement—"be your own story, use your life as a class"—resonated within me and encouraged me to pen my experiences. If I were to give this master class a name, it would be "Miracles 101," and the class description would read: In this class, you will experience the manifestation of God almighty.

Your belief in the manifestation of God's glory means that you trust and have confidence in Him, and you can walk in the authority of His word—as Matthew 18:18 states, "Truly I tell you, whatever you bind on earth will be bound in heaven, and whatever you loose on earth will be loosed in heaven." It's important to understand that the manifestation of the glory of God in your life has everything to do with the place the word of God has in your life, period.

My heart has always been fueled by the words of the Evangelist Luke: "Give, and it will be given to you: good measure, pressed down, shaken together, and running over will be put into your bosom. For with the same measure that you use, it will be measured back to you," Luke 6:38 (NKJV). I've also adopted the words of Martin Luther King Jr. as my mantra: "If I can help somebody as I pass along, if I can cheer somebody with a word or song, if I can show somebody he's traveling wrong, then my living will not be in vain."

It took some time for me to realize my purpose in this life. However, since it has been revealed, I've consistently worked toward walking in it daily. My purpose is my mantra. I fulfill it by sharing my life experiences, both good and bad — as I know the purpose of every one of my experiences and lessons is to help someone else. We are all here for a reason. Do not let the "unknown" spark fear in your spirit. I encourage you to take the unknown as a new class and learn from the experiences.

– Angela E. Thomas-DuPree, Ed.D.

MY STORY

[She] who walks in integrity walks securely ...

Proverbs 10:9

1980: HUMBLE BEGINNING

The phrase "humble beginnings" is an understatement when describing my childhood. I grew up in Labadieville, one of the smallest towns in Louisiana, located along Bayou Lafourche with a population of 1,811 and a total area of 3.9 square miles in Assumption Parish. My family alone made up 1.5 percent of that population with my mother being one of thirteen siblings, and she and my father added twelve to their union.

Growing up, my mind and soul longed for a successful and purpose-filled life far from the low social-economic environment that surrounded me.

It was my mother who taught me to worship and praise God for what I had and to always be thankful. So, before I began to pray for a way out of my situation, I thanked God for life, health, and strength. To this day, the only things I ask God for are wisdom and knowledge. I can still hear my mother's prayer, as she would often quote Matthew 6:25-27:

Therefore I say unto you, take no thought for your life, what ye shall eat, or what ye shall drink; nor yet for your body, what ye shall put on. Is not the life more than meat, and the body than raiment? [26] Behold the fowls of the air: for they sow not, neither do they reap, nor gather into barns; yet your heavenly Father feedeth them. Are ye not much better than they? [27] Which of you by taking thought can add one cubit unto his stature?

After hearing that, there's no need to ask for anything else.

***

Being the youngest of twelve siblings gave way to an easier life than my older siblings, as I learned what to do and what *not* to do amid my mother's authoritative discipline. My mother, Carlbertha Thomas, was the disciplinarian and the boss of everyone. Although I messed up from time to time, I received leniency as the baby of the family. My father, Peter Thomas, was a mild-mannered and happy-go-lucky man, and he gave my mother free rein. She said what she meant and meant what she said, and she did not speak twice.

Although my mother nor father finished high school, they made graduating a priority in our home. Their expectations pushed me to not only take my time at Assumption High School seriously but to also excel in every area that I possibly could throughout those years. I was a part of the track team, a cheerleader for 4 years (serving as a 3-year co-head cheerleader), and the 1980 Homecoming Court 1st Maid. Although the football team initially elected me as queen, they were forced to vote again—and the new results did not include a Black queen.

As I approached high school graduation, I asked my mother if there was any money for me to go to college. "You better find a husband like your sisters," she replied. I was disappointed but also fueled. With none of my eleven siblings having gone to college, I was on my own in the process of preparing to enroll. This is where my "faith" kicked in.

FAITH

Faith was being developed in me (and my siblings) every time Mama made us go to church when we didn't want to. Romans 10:17: *So then faith comes by hearing, and hearing by the word of God.* Faith is to believe God's work in the very essence of receiving the promises that He says we can have. His promise to me was written long before I was born. Philippians 4:19: *But my God shall supply all your need according to his riches in glory by Christ Jesus.*

I know this to be true as my father and mother raised a family of twelve on my father's sugar mill job salary and my mother's maid income. Yet, we never missed a home-cooked meal, and we always had clothes—beautiful, homemade clothes that were sometimes made from the fabric that wrapped the flour Mama used to make her signature rising bread.

Despite every challenge, we were happy. With faith and gratitude, we made it.

LET'S EXAMINE YOUR FAITH.

1. Do you believe in God? If so, what do you believe? Are your beliefs based on biblical scriptures?

2. Describe acting on your faith. What does it look like?

3. When you ask in faith, are you praying God's will? (1 John 5:14-15)

*Conscience is the manifestation of our divine
nature, the absolute truthfulness that we all have
inside, that resides beyond the instinctive desire to survive.*

– IIchi Lee

1981: STRONG DESIRE

In my brother's old, souped-up Monte Carlo, I could barely see the road. The car was raised embarrassingly high from the big tires he'd put on the front. To make matters worse, the engine noise announced my arrival five minutes before I actually reached my destination. Yet, headstrong like my mother—the type to never take *no* for a final answer—I pulled up to Nicholls State University in Thibodaux, LA, approximately 9.1 miles from my hometown. *(This is where Romans 10:17 came into play in my life.)*

Unlike most teens who have dreams of going to college, I didn't have the luxury of leaning on my parents or older siblings for help through the college preparation and enrollment process. I had "a wing and a prayer". If you don't know what "a wing and a prayer" means, it's hoping that you will succeed at something knowing that you're not prepared enough for it. (Insert praise break. *But God!*)

> *Now faith is the substance of things hoped for, the evidence of things not seen.*
> – Hebrews 11:1

Upon my arrival at the university, I was lost. *What am I supposed to do now?* I thought to myself. *Lord help me.* I felt ashamed to show up and not know the first thing to do. *What am I even doing here?* I wondered. Thankfully, Philippians 4:13 popped into my mind and overpowered that thought. Standing in this unfamiliar place trying to decode my next steps, it was all I had to lean on.

Before long, I caught the eye of a sophomore football player who then felt compelled to walk over.

"Can I —" he started.

"Yes!" I blurted out before he could finish the question.

I needed help, and I couldn't waste time being embarrassed about it any longer. He volunteered to walk me through the entire registration process.

I had plans to register for the Interior Design degree program that day, but after the registrar informed me that they didn't offer it, I settled for the Retail Sales & Merchandise Associate Degree program. Nearing the final steps of registering, I thanked the young man for helping me, and from there, I made my way to the bursar's office.

Now, here's the thing: I had no money to pay for classes and didn't know how this was going to go. Attending college was one of my greatest desires at that time, so I made up my mind not to back down. Pressing my way through with Psalm 37:4 brewing in my soul, I kept walking until I reached the clerk at the Bursar's office front desk.

"Ma'am, is there a payment plan I could apply for?" I asked with no reservations. "I don't have money for my tuition and fees today."

Before the clerk could open her mouth to respond, someone walked out of the office door behind me and called out, "Angela!"

Quickly turning around, I noticed it was Mrs. Betty Elfert, an Associate Professor at the university and my mother's employer.

"What are you doing here?" Mrs. Betty asked, walking over to embrace me.

"Trying to register for school."

"Okay," she smiled, knowing I didn't have the money. "Step into my office."

When I entered her office, there was another professor, Mr. Ralph Morel, sitting in one of her waiting chairs. At the time, I had no idea that both

Mr. Morel and Mrs. Elfert would be essential to my success in college. They both worked with the Upward Bound program, a college preparation program for low-income and first-generation college students.

Taking a seat, the two of them proceeded to ask me questions about my aspirations, goals, and objectives. I gave garbled answers, not fully understanding the point of it. *I just wanted to go to college.* I thought to myself. *Why are they interrogating me?*

It wasn't long before I realized that it was all for my good. Somehow, that payment plan I was going to ask about manifested itself. Mrs. Elfert and Mr. Morel allowed me to pay fifty dollars a week toward a small balance of my tuition and fees. To this day, I don't know how they pulled this off, but I truly believed they paid most of my tuition and fees. Not only was my tuition and fees paid but I was also able to stay on campus for two years.

RECOUNT A TIME WHEN YOU WALKED OUT ON PURE FAITH.

1. Explain the situation.

2. Recount the outcome (good/bad).

3. Did you thank God for the outcome?

Thought is a force – a manifestation of energy –
having a magnet-like power of attraction.

– William Walker Atkinson

1984: A SEASON OF PREPARATION

The struggle was real. Day by day, I would struggle through my academic classes. As I mentioned before, I had no prior knowledge of college preparation, registration, student life, academic expectation, etc. I was totally ill-prepared with no one to mentor me through it. It wasn't until I met Mrs. Pamela LaFont, one of the professors of my vocational courses, that I became more secure in my academics. I consider her my guardian angel.

Behold, I am going to send an angel before you to guard you along the way and to bring you into the place which I have prepared.
– Exodus 23:20

Mrs. Pamela was so nice and always willing to assist me. Once I got through the academics, it was smooth sailing from there, as my skillset in retail sales and merchandise management was developing. Before I knew it, I was finished! I was about to become a first-generation college graduate with an Associate of Science degree. As I announced the news to my mother, she was in disbelief. She didn't understand college.

"How could you be finished so soon?" she asked. I tried to explain the degree levels to her, but to be frank, she really didn't care much. All she knew at the time was that her baby was about to become a college graduate. I could hear her on the phone with her friends. "My baby is graduating from Nicholls State University." I truly believe God prepares you for the blessings He is about to bestow upon you.

Immediately after graduating with my Associate Degree in Retail Sales & Merchandise Management, I was offered a manager's position at Chess King, a men's specialty shop in Southland Mall in Houma, Louisiana.

God has something planned for each of us, and if you are not living in the fulfillment of His plan, then now is the time to prepare.

For we are His workmanship, created in Christ Jesus for good works, which God prepared beforehand so that we would walk in them.
– Ephesians 2:10

This was just the beginning.

**

After three years of working as Store Manager at Chess King's Houma location, my management skills proved worthy of a transfer promotion to one of their higher volume stores on Canal Street in New Orleans, LA. It was a higher volume but also higher shrinkage! After one year, I had the shrinkage under five percent. I soon received a personal call from the District Manager of Loss Prevention to congratulate me on the exemplary performance.

**

The next call from my District Manager Tim Gillogly was to inform me that I would be promoted to Field Training Coordinator. The Field Training Coordinator trained *all* newly hired managers in the district. This experience gave me the courage to move to a larger retailer—Zayre Department Store. During those years, Zayre was a large chain of discount retail stores that operated in the Northeastern, Southern, and Midwestern United States from 1956 to 1990. Shortly after I started working at Zayre's New Orleans location, the chain started to close some of its low-performing locations, and as a result, I was offered a transfer to Miami.

GOD'S PREPARATION

1. How did God prepare you for your blessings?

2. Explain your walk in God's workmanship in your life.

3. How did you put it to work?

---

*For the creation waits in eager expectation for the
manifestation of the sons of God.*

– Romans 8:19

1989: A DESTINATION FOR GROWTH

In February of 1989, I moved to Miami, Florida.

On my way to Florida, I remembered a statement my pastor said: "When you get to your destination, find a place to live and then find a church home." I followed his advice and joined Mt. Carmel Missionary Baptist Church on 17th Ave. and 79th Street. I also decided to embark on the process of changing careers.

While traveling from my apartment in Hollywood, FL, to the store location in Miami every day, I'd pass Florida International University (FIU). By April of 1989, I had enrolled and set off in pursuit of a bachelor's degree. This was a difficult time in my life, as I was in a new environment and had to quickly acclimate to a new culture.

Between 1989 and 1995, I job-hopped a bit—leaving Zayre Department Store to work for J. Byrons Department Store, and from there, going to Mervyn Department Store—*all while* attending

FIU. At times, I grew weary. Aside from trying to successfully juggle a full-time job and college classes, I could not seem to master the mathematics component of the College-Level Academic Skill Test (CLAST). I took the test three times to no avail, and I had no time for a tutor. One night, I asked God to show me the way to accomplishing this feat.

Now, the answer I received from God was puzzling—He showed me that I would have to reteach myself in order to get over this hump.

The next day, I ventured to the library for a middle school math book, where I humbly started on page one. With the next test date approaching, I had to work fast. Once I felt confident, I applied to take the CLAST again. This time, I won! I passed the test, and in April of 1995, I had finally earned my Bachelor of Science in Family and Consumer Science.

Yes, it took me 6 years to graduate from FIU, but I often fueled my spirit with Ecclesiastes 9:11: *The race is not given to the swift nor to the strong but he who endures until the end.*

CONQUERING YOUR FEARS

1. God does not give us a spirit of fear. What do you fear?

2. Research the Bible for God's word regarding "fear not" and record it here.

3. Utilizing the scriptures, explain how you would conquer your fears.

Nothing in life is to be feared, it is only to be understood. Now is the time to understand more, so that we may fear less.

– Marie Curie

1995: GOD'S MANIFESTATION

Two weeks after graduation, I was called by FIU and informed that the Maritime And Science Technology Academy school (commonly referred to as MAST Academy) was looking to hire a Family & Consumer Science teacher for their Culinary Arts program. I was asked to meet with the principal as soon as I could.

Just a few minutes into our dialog, the principal asked, "When can you start?" They were ready for me to begin immediately, and I was thrilled to step into my new teaching career. I was ready to take full advantage of the opportunities in front of me. In my very first year there (1995), I was nominated Rookie Teacher of the Year! On a fast track, I also enrolled in the Family & Consumer Science master's program that same year.

Enjoying such a great start at MAST Academy, I had no idea more favor was about to be bestowed upon me.

In addition to studying toward my master's degree credentials, I also enrolled at Miami Dade Community College's childcare training program, as an add-on to my Family & Consumer Science credentials. During one of the childcare class sessions, the teacher asked me to present the nutrition curriculum to the next class.

As I began my presentation that evening, the teacher's supervisor entered the room to conduct her official observation. Upon seeing her, I stopped my presentation, but she enthusiastically said, "Continue, continue!"

After finishing my nutrition presentation, she asked me to step outside with her. I assumed she was going to state some type of student-teacher violation. To my surprise, she offered me a part-time teaching position in childcare. I accepted the offer with excitement! In this new position, I ended up gaining extensive knowledge and experience regarding the childcare industry.

By April of 1997, I had completed the certification in childcare as well as earned my Master of Science degree, with the Cum Laude academic honor.

She is more precious than jewels, and nothing you desire can compare with her.

– Proverbs 3:15

1999: RELATIONSHIPS

MY DAILY DEVOTION

A strong cup of coffee is never all I need to start my day off right— by any means necessary, I must always have a word from the Lord. For years now, my relationship with the Father has been my priority, and my daily devotional with Him has helped me to put life into perspective. At the end of each day, my gratitude for His grace and mercy are expressed with profound appreciation.

"But seek ye first the kingdom of God, and his righteousness; and all these things shall be added unto you."
– Matthew 6:33

Jesus replied: "Love the Lord your God with all your heart and with all your soul and with all your mind.'"
– Matthew 22:37

Every great relationship in my life points back to the relationship I've first built with the Father.

MY SISTERHOOD

Sisters can have a unique bond. Sometimes, sisterhood is a strong, loving relationship with someone who isn't blood-related. On Friday, March 26, 1999, at 9:46 p.m., I became a part of a dynamic sisterhood of Delta Sigma Theta Sorority, Inc. – Dade County Alumnae Chapter. The sorority is a historically African American Greek-letter sorority founded in 1913 at Howard University by 22 college-educated women dedicated to public service. As I lovingly embraced my newfound sisterhood, I made a vow to myself to always maintain my membership and service, being consistent with both my actions and my finances. I am a Diamond Life Member and a charter member of South Broward Alumnae Chapter, which chartered on April 17, 2009. Without a doubt, these friendships have continued to refresh my soul and be a demonstration of God's favor in my life. (Proverbs 27:9)

MY HUSBAND

On Saturday, May 15, 1999, a few weeks after crossing the burning sands, the sorority was invited to the Omega Psi Phi fraternity's annual picnic. As I parked my car, I was immediately encountered by one of the members. The young man politely introduced himself and began to tell me about his involvement in the fraternity. During the event, he'd walk over, from time to time, to the picnic table where I was seated along with my sorority sisters and spark up a brief dialog; until finally, he got up enough courage to ask me on a date.

Our first two encounters after the picnic were at my church on Sunday, May 23rd, and Sunday, May 30th, as I invited him just to see what his reaction would be.

After our first two dates, we established a relationship. Shortly after, we began to see each other exclusively. In July of that year, he visited my home in Louisiana and he asked my family for my hand in marriage. We were married on December 12, 1999. Yes, only seven months after our first encounter at the picnic.

RELATIONSHIP WITH CHRIST

1. How do you start and end your day?

2. Who do you encourage?

3. How do you share the good news of Jesus Christ?

I am a powerful manifester.
Prepare to meet the vibration. You will manifest the
life that you believe.

– Oprah Winfrey

2000: MY DREAMS & ASPIRATIONS

I became one step closer to my dream of becoming an assistant principal. I earned the Educational Leadership endorsement I needed as well as was accepted into the Assistant Principal Training program. Once I completed the training program, I was granted an interview at both Miami Lakes Educational Center and Lindsey Hopkins Educational Center.

Before I left the interview, I felt the assurance that I would be selected for one of the schools. At that time, I was high on Philippians 4:4-7: *Rejoice in the Lord always; again, I will say, Rejoice. Let your reasonableness be known to everyone. The Lord is at hand; do not be anxious about anything, but in everything by prayer and supplication with thanksgiving let your requests be made known to God. And the peace of God, which surpasses all understanding, will guard your hearts and your minds in Christ Jesus.* My assurance was unbreakable.

After two days of waiting to hear back, I received the news: "Congratulations you are being recommended for Assistant Principal at Miami Lakes Educational Center (MLEC)." In July of 2000, I was afforded the opportunity to become an assistant principal under the training of an exemplary school site administrator, Mr. Noward E. C. Dean. As I learned and assisted him in fulfilling the school's vision and mission, I instantly felt a comfortable sense of belonging at this unique institution. At the time, it was only one of two secondary and postsecondary vocational schools on the same campus, and Mr. Dean successfully supervised both schools, with the vocational school offering thirty-five programs accredited by the Council on Occupational Education. At the end of my first full year as assistant principal, Mr. Dean retired. However, he left me well prepared to continue my tenure at MLEC. My time there proved to be a great 10-year experience.

As I continued my academic endeavors, I had taken the Graduate Record Examination (GRE), in hopes to eventually apply to the doctoral program at FIU. The GRE is a standardized exam used to measure one's aptitude for abstract thinking in the areas of analytical writing, mathematics, and vocabulary. The GRE is commonly used by many graduate schools. *Surely*, I thought. *If I had to reteach myself math, how am I going to accomplish abstract thinking in the areas of analytical writing, mathematics, and vocabulary?* On the first test, I did not receive an acceptable score.

Through it all, I was clear about what God could do. One thing I know for sure: He is always working on my behalf, even when I can't see it.

Encouraged by Isaiah 43:19: *Behold, I am doing a new thing; now it springs forth, do you not perceive it? I will make a way in the wilderness and rivers in the desert, I continued to press my way forward* — I continued to study for the next test. Through general dialog, a friend told me about the GRE waiver for minorities. As I understood it, graduate schools were required to accept 10 percent of its minority candidates that did not earn an acceptable score on the GRE. Because of this (and a strong letter of recommendation from my professor), I was able to petition FIU, and soon after, I was granted acceptance to the doctoral program.

After 10 years of a long commute to FIU's south campus and successfully completing two courses toward the doctoral program, I decided to transfer to Nova Southeastern University (NSU). My studies at NSU proved to be enlightening, challenging, and full of rigor. At NSU, I developed strong strategic planning skills and operation compliance methodology.

As I continued my tenure at MLEC, on a typical day at the office, I received a call from my line director informing me that I was being considered for the vice principal's position at the same school. Ending the phone call, I begin to thank God for yet another unseen blessing!

GOD'S UNMERITED FAVOR

1. How do you define God's grace?

2. How has God's favor changed your life?

3. Do you need a dose of God's favor?

Using the following scriptures, pray over yourself:

- 2 Peter 1:2 — *May grace and peace be multiplied to you in the knowledge of God and of Jesus our Lord.*

- Psalm 5:12 — *Surely, Lord, you bless the righteous; you surround them with your favor as with a shield.*

- Romans 5:8 — *But God demonstrates his own love for us in this While we were still sinners Christ died for us.*

- Ephesians 2:8 — *For by grace are ye saved through faith; and that not of yourselves: [it is] the gift of God.*

ANSWERED PRAYERS

As I approached the time to prepare to take the doctoral comprehensive exam, I prayed to God to give me some dedicated time to prepare for the exam. In hindsight, I now understand to be very careful and specific when petitioning God. He will give you exactly what you ask for.

God manifested my request for dedicated time to study through a sudden shift change. Mark 11:24 instructs us how to pray in a certain way: *Therefore I tell you, whatever you ask in prayer, believe that you have received it, and it will be yours.* Although this was an unwanted shift change, in hindsight, it was made clear that God answered my prayer.

My shift was changed from a morning shift to

an evening shift. Miami Lakes Educational Center's morning shifts consisted of operating two schools, the secondary 1,000+ member student body and the postsecondary 700+ member student body. On the other hand, the evening shift enrollment at the time was between 75 and 100 students who were dedicated and focused. This shift gave way to a quiet and challenge-free night. It also allowed me to have dedicated time to study. Although this exact shift-change wasn't what I initially wanted, God had answered my prayer.

As I became confident with the knowledge of my studies, I registered for the doctoral comprehensive exam. On the day of the test, I arrived and proceeded directly to my assigned room. The exam room was very intimidating. The professor enters your assigned room to search through your belongings and computer before issuing the exam. Each student is given four hours to address one, three-part question. I utilized all four of those hours, resulting in an eleven-page answer.

GOD'S MANIFESTATION THROUGH PRAYER

1. What is your prayer?

2. How did God manifest your prayer request?

3. How did you receive your answer?

The life you want is a manifestation of self-realization.

– Bryant McGill

2003: GOD'S GIFTS & GRACE

As I continued my studies at Nova Southeastern University (NSU), my goal was to earn my doctorate degree (Ed.D.) by age 40. My birth date (March 4th) had come and gone as I awaited one signature from my doctorial review team. To my surprise, the final signature was affixed on Monday, March 31, 2003. *To God be the glory!* God continued to bless me! With great excitement, I informed my long-time mentor, Mrs. Elfert, of my accomplishment.

A few months later, Mrs. Elfert nominated me for the Outstanding Alumni Award at Nicholls State University. This award is given to an alumnus who has demonstrated outstanding accomplishments against all odds. It is one of the university's most prestigious awards. This was a demonstration of God's grace. What is grace? Grace is favor, unmerited favor. Grace is what God does because He is gracious. Every action of

God toward us involves His grace. Because of His love, He saved us by His grace.

Grace is a gift from our heavenly Father, given through His son, Jesus Christ. The word grace refers primarily to enabling power and spiritual healing offered through the mercy and love of Jesus Christ. Hebrews 4:16, states: *Let us then approach God's throne of grace with confidence, so that we may receive mercy and find grace to help us in our time of need.*

***

The next few years were the most joyful years of my life. In September of 2004, I gave birth to twin boys, and in October 2005, I gave birth to a beautiful baby girl. Returning to work after two consecutive maternity leaves, not only did I realize just how expensive childcare really was but I also walked into unexpected news. I hadn't fully settled in after returning to work when the principal instructed me to close the school's off-campus childcare training program. This news was supposed to sadden me, but I immediately saw an opportunity on the other side of it. At home that evening, I told my husband what happened with excitement in my voice.

"How is this good news?" he responded, confused at my expression.

"I think we can open our own childcare business!" I announced. My eight years of teaching the childcare program at Miami Dade College would prove to be invaluable.

From that moment forward, my husband was supportive of my first business venture. We opened our first childcare center in 2006, and our kids were the first enrollees. (*What a blessing in financial savings!*) You do the math: Three kids at $150.00 per child per week equals a whopping $1,800.00 per month. This was more than our mortgage payment!

As the first center successfully grew, we opened a second center in 2007 and third in 2011. God's demonstration of Ephesians 2:10 stood profound in our life: *For we are His workmanship, created in Christ Jesus for good works, which God prepared beforehand so that we would walk in them.* God's preparation afforded us years of financial stability.

GOD'S SPIRITUAL GIFTS

1. What are the spiritual gifts and the fruits of the spirit?

2. What is the difference between gifts and grace?

3. What is the power of God's grace?

And I will make them and the places round about my hill a blessing; and I will cause the shower to come down in his season; there shall be showers of blessing.

– Ezekiel 34:26

2012: SHOWERS OF BLESSINGS

I have always enjoyed the rain. The smell of the first drops of rain on dry dirt smells refreshing, and it always makes me smile. I know once the rain starts to shower down, Mama would have us gather the ingredients to make her famous popcorn balls. I don't know what smells the most comforting: the start of the rain or the cooking of the syrup that would be carefully poured into the popcorn. Mama would then scoop a good amount of the popcorn in her hands and squeeze it together to form the delicious balls. As a kid, one thing I knew for sure was that Mama would make popcorn balls *every* time it rained. Despite some disappointments along the way, God has showered me with blessings after blessings.

The year 2012 proved to be another blessed year. I was comfortably working in my appointed position of vice principal, and ironically, I was called into the principal's office on a rainy morning. When I walked in, she was dancing in her chair.

"What's going on?" I asked, smiling but slightly confused.

"You are to report to the supervisor's office immediately!" she yelled out excitedly.

On my drive to the district's office, my mind wandered all over the place. I walked in and courteously greeted my supervisor and another young lady in his office. Not taking the time to engage in any small talk, they got right to the point.

"You are being recommended for appointment to a principal's position."

To be honest, I was not surprised at the recommended appointment. Why? Because I knew God was not finished with me yet.

I thanked them both for their confidence in me and for the recommendation, and I returned to my school thrilled about an even greater opportunity as an educator. My principal was waiting at the entrance, ready to embrace me with a huge hug and *congratulations.*

As the day progressed, I finally received the official call from the district stating that the recommendation was approved by the school board. "Angela E. Thomas-DuPree approved appointed Principal, to (what was then) D. A. Dorsey Educational Center."

This institution is a historical landmark as the land was donated to Miami-Dade County Public Schools by Dania Albert Dorsey (1872-1940), who was born a sharecropper's son. Mr. Dorsey donated the property at NW 71st Street and 17th Avenue on which Dorsey High School was later built, which is currently D. A. Dorsey Technical College. The accredited institution offers career certificate programs in the fields of general education, architecture/construction, health care industry, and transportation, distribution & logistics.

This position has afforded a myriad of experiences and opportunities to help thousands. Not only do I oversee the operation of my assigned school but I also consult clients through the process of establishing their own schools as well as acquiring candidacy, accreditation, or reaffirmation.

RECOUNT YOUR SHOWERS OF BLESSINGS HERE:

1. What are the blessings of the Lord for you?

2. What does God say about blessing others?

3. What are spoken blessings?

Prayer is the atmosphere of revelation, in the strict and central sense of that word. It is the climate in which God's manifestation bursts open into inspiration.

– Peter Forsyth

2013: MY LIVING SHALL NOT BE IN VAIN

I believe teaching is the noblest profession of influence, as is a school administrator.

As I began my principalship, the school was located in an economically distressed community with many challenges. My mantra was realized by the opportunities I saw to assist the community. The community proved to be devastated by poverty and in desperate need of a quality, educational institution equipped to deliver quality workforce development programs.

During my first 18 months, I was deeply involved in the accreditation reaffirmation preparation of the school. The reaffirmation team granted us a six-year approval with no findings of non-compliance and two commendations. This exemplary rating afforded me the opportunity to join the accreditation commission team of reviewers. Since joining, I have traveled throughout the USA with a team of educational professionals reviewing schools for accreditation and/or reaffirmation. This experience has afforded me the knowledge to consult in this field.

I have held the position of Principal at this school for eight years now. Each time I encounter a new enrollee from the community, particularly someone in their 30s or even their 40s, seeking to train for a new career or simply complete high school, I think about my first experience enrolling at Nicholls State University.

With this position, I can truly fulfill my purpose— and with it, my living shall not be in vain.

WHAT MATTERS THE MOST

1. Are you seeing life from God's view?

2. What do you see for your life?

3. How are you ensuring your living will not be in vain? What's your purpose?

Give yourself permission to live a big life. Step into who you are meant to be. Stop playing small. You're meant for greater things.

– Nikhil Garg

TODAY: THE JOURNEY CONTINUES, STEP BY STEP

Allow God's word to manifest in your life. Your existence in this world is on purpose. The word of God offers many insights into man's purpose on earth. Understand that our purpose in life is the very meaning of our existence. Without this, we suffer ignorant of our own significance, and we fall prey to the illusion that our lives don't matter. Without this, we have no connection or impact on the world around us.

But, as it is written, "What no eye has seen, nor ear heard, nor the heart of man imagined, what God has prepared for those who love him.
– 1 Corinthians 2:9.

As I reflect on Oprah's Master Class with J. K. Rowling, the author of Harry Potter, I remember Oprah explaining Rowling's story of "rags to riches". From poor and nearly homeless, Rowling became the world's first billionaire author. Oprah summed up Rowling's entire story in her closing remarks: "Find a way to allow the truth of yourself to express itself. We are all looking for the highest, fullest expression of ourselves as human beings. Unless we are finding a way for what we believe to be true about ourselves to express and manifest itself in the world, we are not living our fullest lives."

God has given us everything. We only have to position ourselves to receive.

Every one of my experiences has given me (what continues to be my prayer to God) the wisdom and knowledge I needed to establish my own consulting business. I currently consult in the areas of college planning and admission for first-generation students, childcare business startup, school accreditation and reaffirmation, and establishing and opening proprietary schools — *to God's glory!*

A PRAYER — LIVING YOUR LIFE FORWARD

Through the experiences I have shared with you in this book, I pray, in some way, that you will be able to experience God's manifestation in *your* life.

As you allow God to work in you, I pray that He helps you live your life in a forward posture. And as you embark on your journey, I pray that He will provide the clarity you seek to articulate the vision for your life.

I pray that you will be fully awake to the realities of the world around you in order to make sound and informed decisions.

Living forward will give you a clear vision and heighten your beliefs in God's words and in what is possible for your life.

Now, pray this for yourself:

Father,

I pray that I experience your manifestation in my life.

As I allow you to work in me, I ask you to help me live my life in a forward posture. And as I embark on this journey, I pray that you provide the clarity I need to articulate the vision for my life.

I pray that I am fully awakened to the realities of the world around me in order to make sound and informed decisions.

I know that living forward will give me a clear vision and heighten my beliefs in your words and in what is possible for my life.

Amen.

MY SONGS OF PRAISE

"IF I CAN HELP SOMEBODY"

If I can help somebody as I pass along,
If I can cheer somebody with a word or a song,
If I can show somebody he is traveling wrong,
Then my living shall not be in vain!

Then my living shall not be in vain,
Then my living shall not be in vain!
If I can help somebody as I pass along,
Then my living shall not be in vain!

If I can do my duty as a Christian oft,
If I can bring back beauty to a world up wrought,
If I can spread love's message that the Master
taught,
Then my living shall not be in vain!

Then my living shall not be in vain,
Then my living shall not be in vain!

If I can help somebody as I pass along,
Then my living shall not be in vain!

1

"OVERCOMER"

How many of you guys are thankful for the blood
of Jesus
So grateful for his blood
(Chorus)
Overcomer, am an overcomer
By the blood of the lamb
And by the word of my testimony
He saved me
He rescued me
He delivered me
And he set me free
Ever since have been changed
Have never been the same
And I can lift my hands and say
Thank you for your grace
(Back to Chorus)
Testimony, I am a testimony
Testimony, this is the word of my testimony
(Back to Chorus)

Overcomer, more than a conqueror
Am a winner, the joy of the Lord is my strength
I have dominion, and I work in authority
Have been, washed in the blood
Am kept by his love
Am filled with his spirit
And by his stripes, am Healed, am Free
Yes! Jesus gave me the victory
(Back to Chorus)
Overcomer!

1

1. Artist: Eddie James (feat. Joe L. Barnes & Jason Gabbard

"GREAT IS THY FAITHFULNESS"

Great is Thy faithfulness
O God my Father
There is no shadow of turning with Thee
Thou changest not
Thy compassions they fail not
As Thou hast been
Thou forever will be
Great is Thy faithfulness
Great is Thy faithfulness
Morning by morning new mercies I see
And all I have needed Thy hand hath provided
Great is Thy faithfulness
Lord unto me
Pardon for sin
And a peace that endureth
Thine own dear presence to cheer
And to guide
Strength for today

and bright hope for tomorrow
Blessings all mine, with ten thousand beside
Great is Thy faithfulness
Great is Thy faithfulness
Lord every morning new mercies I see
And all I have needed Thy hands hath
provided
Great is Thy faithfulness
Great is Thy faithfulness
Great is Thy faithfulness
Lord unto me
So faithful too me

1

1. Artist: Chris Rice; Composer: Thomas Chisholm / W.M. Runyan

"AMAZING GRACE"

Amazing Grace, how sweet the sound
That saved a wretch like me
I once was lost, but now am found
Was blind but now I see

Was Grace that taught my heart to fear
And Grace, my fears relieved
How precious did that Grace appear
The hour I first believed

Through many dangers, toils and snares
We have already come
T'was Grace that brought us safe thus far
And Grace will lead us home
And Grace will lead us home

Amazing Grace, how sweet the sound
That saved a wretch like me

I once was lost but now am found
Was blind but now I see
Was blind, but now I see

1

"SPEAK THE NAME"

The atmosphere is changing
Nothing stays the same
Heaven is waiting
For the mention of the Name
The Spirit is moving
Burning like a flame
Healing the broken
By the One we proclaim
Raise it up
Fill the sky
Chains will fall
Mountains move
We lift Him high
Speak the Name
The Name above all other names
Speak the Name
The Name the wind and waves obey
All of heaven's coming down
Fill the earth with the sound

Of the Name
The Name of Jesus
Gather all who wonder
Hostages of shame
Miracles unfolding
At the mention of the Name
Our darkness is fleeing
Mercy raining down
Healing waters flowing
As our lips make the sound
Raise it up
Fill the sky
Chains will fall
Mountains move
We lift Him high
Speak the Name
The Name above all other names
Speak the Name
The Name the wind and waves obey
All of heaven's coming down
Fill the earth with the sound
Of the Name
The Name of Jesus
Speak the Name
The Name of Jesus
Strongholds are broken
I've been made free

I am forgiven
Fear has to leave
Strongholds are broken
I've been made free
I am forgiven
Fear has to leave
Your Name is healing
Your Name is power
Your Name is holy
My strong, strong tower
Wonderful Name
Glorious Name
Powerful Name of Jesus
Jesus
Speak the Name
The Name above all other names
Speak the Name
The Name the wind and waves obey
All of heaven's coming down
Fill the earth with the sound
Of the Name
The Name of Jesus
Of the Name
The Name of Jesus
Speak the Name
The Name of Jesus

1

1. Composers: Aaron W. Lindsey / Bernie Herms / Koryn Hawthorne; © Universal Music Grp, Essential Music Pub., Capitol Christian Music Grp

"HOW GREAT THOU ART"

O Lord my God,
When I in awesome wonder
Consider all
The works Thy Hand hath made,
I see the stars,
I hear the mighty thunder,
Thy power throughout
The universe displayed,
When through the woods
And forest glades I wander
I hear the birds
Sing sweetly in the trees,
When I look down
From lofty mountain grandeur
And hear the brook
And feel the gentle breeze,
Then sings my soul,
My Savior God, to Thee,
How great Thou art!

How great Thou art!
Then sings my soul,
My Savior God, to Thee,
How great Thou art!
How great Thou art!
When Christ shall come,
With shouts of acclamation,
And take me home,
What joy shall fill…

1

1. Artist: Chris Rice; Composer: Carl Boberg

"WAY MAKER"

You are here, moving in our midst
I worship You
I worship You
You are here, working in this place
I worship You
I worship You
You are here, moving in our midst
I worship You
I worship You
You are here, working in this place
I worship You
I worship You
You are
Way maker, miracle worker, promise keeper
Light in the darkness
My God, that is who You are
You are
Way maker, miracle worker, promise keeper

Light in the darkness
My God, that is who You are
You are here, touching every heart
I worship You
I worship You
You are here, healing every heart
Healing every heart
Oh, I worship You
Jesus, I worship You
You're turning lives around
You are here, oh, turning lives around
I worship You
I worship You
You mended every heart
You are here, and You are mending every heart
I worship...

1

"BREAK EVERY CHAIN"

There is power in the name of Jesus / There is
power in the name of Jesus / There is power in
the name of Jesus
To break every chain, break every chain, break
every chain
To break every chain, break every chain, break
every chain
There is power in the name of Jesus / There is
power in the name of Jesus / There is power in
the name of Jesus
To break every chain, break every chain, break
every chain
To break every chain, break every chain, break
every chain
There is power in the name of Jesus / There is
power in the name of Jesus / There is power in
the name of Jesus
To break every chain, break every chain, break
every chain

To break every chain, break every chain, break
every chain
There's an army rising up / There's an army
rising up / There's an army rising up
To break every chain, break every chain, break
every chain
To break every chain, break every chain, break
every chain
There's an army rising up / There's an army
rising up / There's an army rising up
To break every chain, break every chain, break
every chain
To break every chain, break every chain, break
every chain
There's an army rising up / There's an army
rising up / There's an army rising up
To break every chain, break every chain, break
every chain
To break every chain, break every chain, break
every chain
I hear the chains falling / I hear the chains
falling

1

1. Artist: Tasha Cobbs; Composers: Will Reagan

"NEVER GIVE UP"

Visions that can change the world
Trapped inside an ordinary girl
She looks just like me
To afraid to dream out loud
And though it's set for your idea
It won't make sense to everybody
You need courage now
If you're going to persevere
To fulfill your divine purpose
You've gotta answer when you're called
So don't be afraid to face the world
Against all odds
Keep the dream alive don't let it die, if some-
thing deep inside
Keeps inspiring you to try, don't stop
And never give up; don't ever give up on you
Don't give up
Every victory comes in time
Work today to change tomorrow

It gets easier
Who's to say that you can't fly?
Every step you take you gets
Closer to your destination
You can feel it now
Don't you know you're almost there?
To fulfill your life's purpose
You've gotta' answer when you're called
So don't be afraid to face the world
Against all odds
Keep the dream alive don't let it die, if some-
thing deep inside
Keeps inspiring you to try, don't stop
And never give up; don't ever give up on you
Sometimes life can place a stubborn block in
your way
But you've gotta keep the faith
Reap what deep inside your heart
To fly
And never give up
Don't ever give up on you,
Don't give up
Who holds the pieces to complete the puzzle?
The answer that can solve the mystery
The key that can unlock your understanding
It's all inside of you
You have everything you need
So, keep the dream alive don't let it die

If something deep inside keeps inspiring you to
try
Don't stop
And never give up; don't ever give up on you
Sometimes life can place a stubborn block on
your way
But you've gotta keep the faith
Bring what's deep inside your heart
To the light
And never give up
Don't ever give up on you
No don't give up
No, no, no, no
Don't give up
Don't give up
Don't give up
Oh, don't, no, no, no, no
Don't, give, up

1

1. Artist: Yolanda Adams; Composers: Yolanda Yvette Adams, James
Harris III, Terry Lewis, James Wright

ABOUT THE AUTHOR

Angela E. Thomas-DuPree, Ed.D. is a native of Labadieville, Louisiana, and the twelfth child of Peter and Carlbertha Thomas. She currently resides in Ft. Lauderdale, Florida, with her husband Clyde S. DuPree and their three kids—twins, Jason and Justin, and beautiful daughter, Jenesis.

She earned her associate's degree in 1984 from Nicholls State University. In 1995, she earned her bachelor's degree, and in 1997, she earned her master's degree from FIU with the Cum Laude academic honor. In 2003, she earned her Ed.D. from Nova Southeastern University.

Dr. Thomas-DuPree has been an administrator for over 21 years with the Miami-Dade County School System. Her love for education affords her the opportunity to foster students' endeavors daily. She is an educational entrepreneur, as she was the owner and operator of three successful childcare centers, and has plans to launch her independent educational academy as her retirement endeavor.

Dr. Thomas-DuPree loves helping others, serving the community, and serving her church. She is a Diamond Life member of Delta Sigma Theta Sorority, Inc. and a charter member of the South Broward Alumnae Chapter of Delta Sigma Theta Sorority, Inc., where she served as a charter officer and continues to be actively involved.

She has received the Outstanding Alumni honor from Nicholls State University and also named one of Legacy Magazine's Top Black Educator of 2016. She has received the South Broward Alumnae Chapter of Delta Sigma Theta Sorority, Inc. Fortitude Award for 2010-2011, as well as service award recognitions from the Urban League of Greater Miami for Outstanding Leadership in Education and D. A. Dorsey Technical College Black History – Legacy Honors for Educational Contributions.

People often say life does not come with a manual. I beg to differ. The Holy Bible is your manual:

The Commandment
Deuteronomy 30:16

The Instruction
Colossians 3:23-24

The Guidance
Proverbs 13:3, 19:8, and 21:21

The Declaration
John 6:35

The Reward
Ephesians 1:11

Made in the USA
Columbia, SC
10 July 2020